WAITING FOR SWEET BETTY

Waiting for Sweet Betty

Clarence Major

 Copper Canyon Press

Some of these poems previously appeared in the following periodicals:

Callaloo
Journal of Literature and Aesthetics (India)
PreviewPort (a Web site)
Smart Pace

Copper Canyon Press is in residence under the auspices of the Centrum Foundation at Fort Worden State Park in Port Townsend, Washington. Centrum sponsors artist residencies, education workshops for Washington State students and teachers, Blues, Jazz, and Fiddle Tunes Festivals, classical music performances, and the Port Townsend Writers' Conference.

LIBRARY OF CONGRESS CATALOGING-IN-PUBLICATION DATA

Major, Clarence.
Waiting for sweet Betty / Clarence Major.
 p. cm.
ISBN 1-55659-179-9 (alk. paper)
1. Title.
PS3563.A39 W35 2002
811'.54 — DC21

2002013392

9 8 7 6 5 4 3 2 FIRST PRINTING

COPPER CANYON PRESS
Post Office Box 271
Port Townsend, Washington 98368
www.coppercanyonpress.org

Contents

WAITING FOR SWEET BETTY

Part One

San Diego and Matisse

1. INSIDE FROM THE PERSPECTIVE OF A TREE

Beautiful women in smoky blue culottes
lying around on fluffy pink pillows
beneath windows onto charming views,
sea views, seasonal leaves and trees.
Inside is outside and outside inside.
Smell of saltwater swimming in the room.

2. OUTSIDE FROM THE PERSPECTIVE OF A ROCKING CHAIR

Shadow of lighthouse along the beach.
Whales spotted every day lately
though winter's two months yet.
The evening is as warm as an interior.
Silverlight lagoonlight, snorkeling light.
And a line of joggers against last light.
Blue smoke snaking up the pink sky.

Mendocino

I could lose myself in great bursts of work
here, cutting wood, planting a garden, painting
what I see, or I could get lazy
on our marine terrace. First and last. I want to last.

We stand on ground mapped since 1587, a long time
for this our country and what did Lorenzo do
here? Or for that matter, Antonio? Colony and cove comfort.

Fog every morning obscuring coastline. You
need a warm sweater and you come out of it by noon.
Victorian rows along unpainted lanes,
we walk searching for everything and nothing in
particular. Agate, Blair, Caspar, Lansing, etc.

Off One, with groceries in trunk, enough
to last till next trek ten miles south to
ex-fortress. Put frozen stuff away
first. Sun only halfway down. Still time
to catch its effect and handcraft it to
something reusable like leftovers,
bouillabaisse perhaps.

Rock and a Hard Place

A tough day on the mesa.
Sawmill smoke roving this way.

Roughly we're between Modoc and Modesto,
mission incomplete.

Animals killed here, rotted back
into the earth's terms. Being and nothingness,
a long time ago in my youth, Sartre: you
go back where you came from.
Worms worked their way on remains
in this arid region. You
can laugh and say life is a joke, but

a severe fight goes on in its good name,
since a beginning, and we survive
doubts of an ending.

Vizcaino

Here at Cape Vizcaino in Mendocino

we stop not so much today

to commemorate Sebastián

but to gaze out at something

just below sky

and just above ocean.

It's a human heart beating?

No, it's a volcanic plug or a knob.

Or perhaps a point of conception

too abstract to identify further,

but it gives me an idea — I scribble

on the postcard we bought yesterday:

Dear Sybil: Vis-kay-noh's atmosphere

is a floating vineyard of visitations,

not necessarily holy or whole, but

the fog lifts by noon

and what passes for reality returns.

Take care. See you soon.

Art Is Parallel to Nature

Cézanne saw the parallel so well and

connected the green to the stone so well.

This day we are in Santa Clara

driving low among high trees, cedar green.

It's a paradise site of ancient dreams

illuminated by rain flung down thinly

and wet trunks bloody red.

And road after road so connected,

and connected too to undergrowth

as the folded arms of day complain, descending.

Yet light still comes through brush

high and flat, as night hugs Morro Rock.

And we arrive to see believers

bent in posture of penitence

waiting for reinvigoration.

From the Train Window Going and Coming

I ride backwards to see what I'm missing.

Big pines and big skies ride up and down and around,
up and down and around then for a straight stretch.

A white pickup shooting along a white highway east with us.

Note I'm trying to call home but cannot.

Sky and brush and pine and salt-earth curving sharply, tilting away...

The window opens to a large natural tallness.

In the great distance blue mountain comfort...

In the middle distance of Winnemucca a darkness coming...

In the near distance of Granby a sentimental stretch nearly missed...

We are stopping by a pasture and one cow gazes at us while
two hundred cows remain interested only in grazing.

I look forward to going back, either way.

Winter in Northern California

When is Chicago not too cold or too hot?

Snow, wet slabs of it piled up around the house.

... Here in sun-splashed California, seeing Chicago
behind a freezing reporter...

Let all the leaves fall unregistered.

Winter summer spring – ring the bell.

But then there was spring.
In good weather, whether or not it was the right thing,
I played in the sandbox, played hooky, played marbles,
played the dozens, played up and down the block,
played Pin the Tail on the Donkey, played myself out.

Play itself curves away from us like the sky as we get older.

People are cheering in the plaza because the rain is stopping.

What you wear in the parade, though, doesn't much matter
since bodies are close together where warmth is willful.

Like the man said, just keep stepping to the trumpet,
or at least keep kissing in the doorway.

Summer Place: Cambria

I'm out front, first light spotted
me and attached itself. Sunny and breezy already this
morning, on morning-side of house. I want
to paint the big tree but something in me is not ready, so
these are my brushstrokes. Wind chimes on deck moving.
Empty birdbath. Black vulture circling above ocean's edge.
Gray hawk in blue tree. Bald eagle standing
on fence. Wingspan ninety inches if a foot.
He heads for the big bottleneck down cliffside.
I take the path around to the back deck.
I'm both drained of and filled with everything.
I try the deck door. Still locked from night's fears of darkness.
Go in through side door. I start water
over flame, my sentinel light glows
in the water, turning it silver like a boiling chandelier.

Habitat: Time and Place

Cambria, California, 1999

This is out by the stand of windbreak-trees, under
the one with the nosy condor.

I'm startled by the brilliance, the resilience
of this summer of hawkweed gone to seed.

Nature's con is chatty and shrill.
Pheasant's eye, Christe herbe, St. John's wort
are too much, too flamboyant for words
but not for birds or splashy weather.
For better or not, this is where we are.

Today, hill pasture, full of flax's white,
same as yesterday, gnarly and snippy.
I'm out here going to seed under the tree.
I'm suspicious of this open land laid out and out.

It's friendly but
unsympathetic—or maybe it's me, maybe it's just me.
I keep framing it anyway
but it goes beyond frame
while staying the same, immodest and lippy.

A few random things out here—
one yellow flower of five petals,

chickweed clumsy and enchanting,
pink powder puff scraggly and scuzzy.
This place decodes me, reloads me.

I stare down the condor, bald head and red neck.
He waits sagely,
measuring distances, measuring curve of sky.
What song will such a bird sing?

He flaps his underwing whites at me,
pecks at a spot on the limb.
As slightly as I am unsightly, he is nobility itself.
Black codes: he sends me his hot signals.
I receive them openheartedly.
Am I sending them back openly?

      It's time. It is time, he says, it's time.

But it doesn't matter.
A butterfly lands on a red camellia.

Nature is taking care of itself and all that matters.
Nature goes.
My presence is a flyspeck on a leaf.
It keeps me down to size.

Gathering Mushrooms: Cambria

A valley and hillside full of helmet-flowers
with that curious upper-sepal shooting out.
Not truly colorless, the color of life itself,
drinking air and spitting acid,
surviving on death, eating its flesh —
mold, mildew, bacteria. More like musk of animal
than smell of vegetable. Stinkhorn stinks yet dry
out a toadstool and the smell is sweet.

The girl's Airedale digs in the hillside,
turning back earth, spreading yeastiness in the air.
Overhead in trees — *stweet-stweet* — a sound securing the day.

She gathers mushrooms on the cliff.
Folk around here say they're stems
of old wives' hoods, friars' caps blowing
in noon's wind, a whiff of death full of life.
The girl insists they're both life and disease,
fertility, too, two by two — too many to count.
At ease, she carries a fistful of shoots,
spindly fleshy things. *They're both life and disease,
two by two. Too many to count.*

Shoreline at Cambria

Early morning shoreline: a scattering of birds blackens the sky. They cover rocks and fill trees. Seabirds. Shorebirds. Yellowlegs. Stilts. Ruddies. Spotteds. Now a ribbon of tiny ones I can't name flying in from sea. Wavy line of gulls flying out to sea. Geese and waders. Lessers. Longers. Surfers. Rock-standing birds arriving. And I'm out standing on the deck trying to capture this but it's not possible.

Moon and Moonlight (at Cambria)

How to dance to your music,
full of swooning and rapture?
Those times are gone.
Bedazzled by you and your light,
swayed by the slap of waves tossing
and lifting to your baton. Gone.

What if I never learn the new steps?
I was always bad at science and math.

After we landed on you and saw there was no man, we lost the
        festive smile and
gained a maniacal caution, gained a vulgar reality.

Very well, stay up in your newness. I take you as you were.
        Empty-headed!
Raffish! Zesty! Spiteful! Love-struck! Cerebral and clear, clever
        and concise,
more mysterious before we touched you, walked our big boots
        on your rocky
range, planted our flag in your nipple.

In the old way, your ripples remain
specific and luminous over black Pacific,
and even now in your borrowed light
I see you waving back
to your old skeptic.

Purple California Mountains

near Half Moon Bay

Late afternoon; see what I can see
from this hillside. I have two views.

Pale blue lake nesting in crevice, the view
while you are waiting in this gray house
we rented yesterday. Red pony chewing blue grass
in the yard, boundaries set by split joint;
I will come inside and wait with you.
These boundaries are made of the simplest things —
gravity closure age cones shingles mimicry,
pigeon cooings blades of grass overlappings.
The naked eyes —
that's a boundary, too, and two, from a window in the house.
The darkness there is not yours, not mine.
Concrete in its promise, corrosive and full of dust, it.
We knew it the moment we entered, we knew.
It's not our darkness, it's rented.

Yet light surrounds the darkness, a light
that connects us to the unknown owners.
On the roof a giant black chimney.
The unseen part reaches down into the living room
hard and straight, absolute in purpose.
If the house burns down it's the single thing
that will remain standing alone in a clearing.

Look the other way:
sea and seaside and sailboats tipping, this energy,
this reminder, this reassurance, this bridge
reaches across with a purpose unmistakable, utilitarian.
It affords necessary passage
from one unmarked place to another.

The inlet letting fishing boats in, way
the other way, in a distance too close to distinguish
from what is at hand; I see
the limits of what I can or will ever.
These boundaries were always.

The Lay of the Land

Half Moon Bay, summer, 1999

Out behind the house land and sea.
Earth sloping off at an angle.
It's wearing a gaggle of trees twisted
and waving in slabs of wind.
Trees don't come in gaggles.
Curve of land visible everywhere
up- and downcoast.
We've driven, we know.
Scattered and giddy shapes,
sea clouds push on and on.
Our windbreakers flapping
as we lean homeward.

Unknown Harbor

Housebound in a house not our own:
the repairman keeps us waiting.
Windows wet
with fog. Boats out there, serious men
fishing the ocean, waiting for a bite.
Their lives no more rented
than ours. Camping in style...
the wait is nevertheless no
shorter than in camp.
If we go out
we miss out surely. Go wait
in line for bay cruise tickets
and see how far we get.

The lesson
here is keep busy with you-know-what.
And that's how you get to Chinatown
for the festival by way of an unknown harbor.

Before and After

It'll take a while they say.
Postponement.
They mean delay.

> The foot and the hand join
> the other foot and hand
> too quickly in celebration.

Waiting in hotel lobbies for contacts.
The play delayed due to... well,
you know. Kafka wasn't the only one.
His day, and today stretched out.

> The second round of music
> isn't heard clearly, and

lady at the market, over her onions,
said it in her own way: That's life.
And Elmer knew too. Look how long
he waited to return to the figure.
And when he did everything turned
natural as crawling, as climbing, as rocks.

> When any note is missed
> tapestry of motion suffers.

So, what do you think?

Book Title: ....

Comments: ....

....

....

Can we quote you on that? ☐ yes ☐ no

Copper Canyon Press seeks to build the awareness of, appreciation of, and audience for a wide range of emerging and established American poets, as well as poetry in translation from many of the world's cultures, classical and contemporary. To receive our catalog, send us this postage-paid card or email your contact information to poetry@coppercanyonpress.org

NAME: ....

ADDRESS: ....

CITY: ....

STATE: .... ZIP: ....

EMAIL: ....

☐ Send me *Editor's Choice*, a bimonthly email of poems from forthcoming titles.

BUSINESS REPLY MAIL

FIRST-CLASS MAIL   PERMIT NO. 43   PORT TOWNSEND WA

POSTAGE WILL BE PAID BY ADDRESSEE

Copper Canyon Press
PO Box 271
Port Townsend, WA 98368-9931

Delay is that stretch
in front of an earthquake.
There I go again. Just like targets
hit. Before they are, you're in
a stretch like a trek, but it's smooth
as coming down in a balloon
into a valley's lap. I could show you
on a map of open space,
but it wouldn't do any good now.

Chinatown Blues

Waiting for the streetcar in San Francisco
like a sightseer, who sees nothing,
I play my favorite mental game.
San Francisco is a cartoon and I am
a cartoon character in this cartoon strip.
When I swear because the streetcar is late,
in the balloon above my head
exclamation marks and stars dance together.
Up there a festival is in progress.
The Chinatown kite shop
has sold out. Grant Avenue
is so jammed you can't move.
I see the streetcar three blocks
away, motionless, stuck in the crowd.
I'm furious.
I open my mouth to speak
and above my head
a second balloon appears,
empty.

The Purchase

Once you've bought into the suspension of disbelief
the tour guide lays suspense on you. And
while you are in that state, he pours all the details – all
the things you are not necessarily interested in – over
you like a rinse after a soaping: all
places named after the abalone in California,
Geodetic Survey reports,
a map of the first route to the Pacific Coast,
a treatise on whaling,
a history of San Mateo.
And before you realize you are irritated
by the delay, you feel pleased to learn
something new and useful.
And so what if it was a trick?
Sometimes it is necessary
to buy a thing you don't want.

Part Two

Van Gogh's Death

We climbed the steep stairway
to the tiny attic death-room,
more alive for doing so.
Are people talking about power of imagination
when they say
Christ died so we may live?

Tall cypresses still waving in the afternoon.
Everywhere people feel deeply
and look closely and carefully at last things.

On the news the oldest woman said,
He was the ugliest man I ever saw.
And I hear him saying to her, Your beauty
like a cypress by the road
more than makes up for what I lack.

And we came down with his life
all around us out there in the fields,
and walked up past the church
to the headstones planted close to the wall.

Rembrandt's Etching of a Woman Pissing

We know the squat.

We know the hastily lifted bundle of skirts
held firmly in potato-hands.

We know sharp eyes
in fearful scrutiny of surroundings.

It's all so natural, it's the animal.

The splash itself — out and up, away —
a clean stream —

life loves life.

Portrait of the Great White Hunter
Foxhunting in the Absence of Big Game

Open the stable gate!
Send out the call!

You're out into the valley
where the tall grass moves in waves
under the electric sun,

my head full of wild dreams of conquest
and cries yet to be released.

In a flat-bottom johnboat: floating blind
with the ducks overhead, their necks stretched
all in one direction flying south.

This is my head.
These words are coming
out of a hole in my head.

An Eighteenth-Century Moment

A young married couple.
A comfortable domestic setting.
Upper-class with expensive china
and glass, gold and green silk, but
furnished in terms of taste poorly.
A waste of money and music.

She wears a secret smile of pleasure.
She's been out all night.
He's been out all night, too.
Their little dog sniffs at the lace panties hanging from his pocket.

I mean only to take this as a point of departure.
This is where I depart,
go my own way, leaving
their shabby elegance
to the rhythm of Haydn.

It's a season but that's not why.
Gaudy figures on the fake-gold mantel.
Piss-poor paintings all the way down the hall.
Tall windows with the best of light.
A broken sword hanging on the wall for no good reason.

An embroidered pattern
of Macedonian reds and greens
in long zigzag competing lines.
This isn't bad but its presence is an accident.
The light gambles with everything.

Carrying an orange fruit bowl full of apples,
the snobbish steward comes and goes
splashed with pink heat.

He will tell you about the smell
of the meat market, how both can't stand
fruit or lute music for that matter,
Macedonia or Haydn quiet or loud.

Looking out the window into the piazza
through midafternoon stillness
caressed and cuddled by the usual steaminess,
I see a midget with stumps
for arms and no thumbs
making his way across from shade to light
where the church entrance stands like a square
of blackness in a dream full of whispers.
He thinks he's unseen.

Here is the altar.
Some are already kneeling.
He will enter the church of spheres and cylinders
and go down on his knees
in the circular dark, unaware

of the girl three seats away,
with a broken weedy heart,
sitting in an unholy unladylike manner,
knees apart, tears zigzagging down her face.

What was it I meant to say about
this pathetic couple in their pathetic life,
and the midget, the piazza light and shadow,
the cool interior of the church?

Ah! Anyway, apples in an orange bowl.
Apples in an orange bowl.
See the light coming from inside each apple
as though holiday candles were glowing
from inside a house?
And on the path of candlelight a band
of noble white mares
galloping out through the red skin,
filling the world with their thunderous music.

Sunday Afternoon

In this season of "sweet
silent thought" on a Sunday afternoon
you both hold hands
and walk the park lanes,
strolling, silent and separate in your thinking,
far away from each other in feeling.
What do you seek and why is it so hard?

Despite your fear, you admire the bright flowers,
brighter than lighted rooms.
Brightness! Great brightness!
Money, time, reputation, honor, none
of these its equal,
for brightness is imagination itself.
A tear rolls down your cheek
but you can still see clearly.

An old man greets you in English,
and using his cane proudly points to a big tree.
"It's over a hundred years old," he says
with great reverence, then
goes off past the black
iron mermaids gracing the stairway
to the walkway along the water.

Years from now when one of you tries to remember
this moment, it will be too sentimental.
Your thoughts, the true reality,
will shimmer as light on water,
in place of this Sunday afternoon in Madrid.
The old man himself will be different,
with a little more style and less pride.
Your thoughts will replace the old tree
with an imaginary tree,
one with its own terms.
That Sunday afternoon's sad silence
will be erased by the brightness you find here.

Edward Hopper's Woman Sitting on the Bed

Holding a glass of water, I looked out the window,
a rear window with shutters.
I saw a row of fenced-off backyards
with clotheslines running
from the rear of the buildings out
to poles at the ends of long strips of yards.

On one line hung a red garter belt
and a pair of green stockings,
and a pink slip danced on the wind.
Nothing on any of the others.

The Red Light District was three blocks down
and across the Civil War memorial park.
It was midafternoon, dark soon, so the big-butt women
were beginning to come out and stand in doorways.

It was past time to call downstairs for the bellhop.
Out on the street somewhere from a portable radio
I heard bebop — Parker after Camarillo, unbelievable.

I glanced over my shoulder
at the woman on the bed.
She gazed and gazed hard at the floor.
Somebody was knocking at the door.

This was all a game somehow.
Years later she would brag about living in a big house
and having lots of money to spend.

A Mountain Village in Southern France

Snow on a line of flat rooftops beneath a sky of driven clouds. Warm for winter. It feels like summer. Below on a cobbled narrow passageway, an old woman in a heavy black coat shuffles along carrying a bread basket. From somewhere within the stone walls a young woman cries out, but not in pain. It's early. A hundred years ago another old woman shuffled along toward the same bakery with a different name located in the same street with the same name. Just like this old woman she was neighborly and merciful, crotchety and cursed, petty and paradoxical, ailing though active. It was this early in the morning on a morning like this. She walked past the same dark entryways, the same locked gateways, past the same skinny dog sniffing piss-stained cobbles, past the same columns and empty scaffolding. She passed beneath the same three verandas in a row. She walked by the churchyard, with its whitewashed stones lining the walkway, and past the lych-gate. She shuffled on across the *cour* and under the archway. Both old women walked at the same pace and wore the same coat. They carried the same straw basket, except the earlier basket had a nice little hinged top and a cast-iron latch. A slight breeze blew in from the nearby sea just like this morning. It came in across a sea of wheat trembling at sunrise, and the wheat blades glowed yellow-white above blue shadows beneath each blade, row after row, with nobody there to appreciate the glory. Loneliness permeated that place as now and the fields and the village. The smell of cypress in the meadow below the fields rode high up through the old stone dwellings, and on up farther to the hills where hermits stayed hidden like bugs beneath doormats in rainy weather.

No One Goes to Paris in August

A Montparnasse August
with view of the Cimetière. A yard of bones.

We wake to it. Close curtains to it.
Wake to its lanes. Rows of coffin-stones in varying light.

Walking here. Late with shade low, low, long.
We're passing through, just passing through
neat aisles of gray mausoleums.

(From Paris. Send this postcard. This one.
Calm water lilies. Water lilies.
Nothing colorless.)

It's morning. Baudelaire's tomb.
Tree limbs casting shadow west.

This, a lot of time under a looming sky.
Nobody has time like this.
(Time to go to Le Mandarin for coffee
every day. We're not complaining.
They bring the milk separate.
Watch the passersby on Saint-Germain.)

Nothing to ponder. This is the plight.
Pause by Pigeon in bed with his wife —
both fully dressed.

Pink flowers, pink flowers,
just beneath de Beauvoir's name.
When she lived she lived two doors down.
Went south in August.

All of us smell of heat all the time.
We are the living. Oh dear!
There are the dead ones there.
Their thoughts more familiar, though.
Lives finished, nearly clear.
And they make it possible for us to go on living
as we do in their blue shade.

Paris Plan in Hand

Every day you are one and I am, too. Paris city-plan in hand, Métro pass in the other. We sit next to a frog-headed goddess. First impression – self as object in space. Tocqueville's first impression of New York as he approached it on the East River: grand stone palaces, but they turned out to be only whitewashed bricks. Tocqueville was one and you are one. Here in Paris we walk to the supermarket and everybody knows we're not from around here. They can tell on sight. Then we open our mouths. People walking along with phones stuck to the sides of their heads, grinning, just like in America. One day couscous in Restaurant Baraka.

In the back room two locals are already eating heartily and chattering away. They are two and we are two. The first few steps are hard anywhere. This side or that. Two different sides of the same dancing. It's anybody's life, that one, this one.

One day in the dungeon, smell of gunnysacks, rotten leaves, mustiness. Then dust of headstones lingering over tracks running on and on. Tree-lined cemetery far as the eye. Children lined up and marched through to see – Baudelaire, Sartre, Brancusi, Beckett. With basket in hand and though far from home we walk to the market in rue Daguerre just like regulars on a regular basis.

Now and then gossip from home arrives by postcard:
"It was about nothing, the breakup."
"Her little son leaped from the shadows
and wrapped the girl in the American flag.

His teacher made him stay after school."
"Robbie and Bobbie got divorced last week."
"Sonny's novel was rejected again."
"I got a cold I can't kick for three weeks now."

Somewhere a motor starts then stops.
Emergency sirens below so often
you come to think the sound natural.
Washing machine in the toilet
also making an awful racket.
All night the traffic on the boulevard
and gas fumes coming up through the open window.
Yet you are in Paris and you love the idea.

Some mornings are fresh and bright
and beyond belief you feel the fullness of it.
Through the window what a relief, trees trembling
against the gray stone of old buildings.
Slap of daylight brings something back to life in you,
even after a sleepless night.

Then again there are days when you are out
of focus and out of sorts,
out of hearing, out on a broken branch.

Then you snap out of it.
Like the day down by the Seine
where an artist was painting the river
with docked boats. You stood and watched her
work and you felt better.
She was painting a view of the Left Bank painted to death
but she put her life in and something happened.

One day you go to meet friends at Café Français at Place de
    la Bastille.
You sip coffee and they sip tea and wine.
The shrine in full view in front of you
with traffic whirling around it.
Ah, this city — continuous variety.

Mornings and midafternoons
your gaze is fixed outward:
your fourth-floor window looking out
at the Jewish section
of the cemetery and beyond at Eiffel.
Hard shadows, yellow trees and hard shadows.
Wish you could stay.

The long stone wall running to the vanishing point,
disappearing into the distant trees.

Enough to take your breath away.
Morning sunlight on rows and rows.
An apartment with a view of death.

Paris. The twins are connected with twine. You are one, I am one.
They're trying to escape each other, but stagnation and entropy
hold them down. "Always equal distribution." Paris. Each to the
other is a secret sharer. Paris twins carry the weight of wakeful-
ness. In Paris you look twice at paintings, sometimes three times
for the reality.

One day last week everybody sat down at the same time.
This was a small, nontourist restaurant,
family menu: you ate what they ate.
Charitable faces all around eating the same.
You were still an other, but they'd taken you in
with compassion and trust.
Later you realized you were practicing
as if for that horizontal tightrope
where the tension is between object and creator.

Then back downstairs to the long curving
stretch of Monet's water lilies.
You stood listening to faint ripples
in reds underneath blues and greens.

At one point you stood briefly
against Le Tournon in memory of Himes.
You stood this time against red over blue.
It was raining that afternoon
and then it was not raining, so
you window-shopped your way back
across the city to your Métro, dropping coins
into the outstretched hands of dead angels.

Remember, I stood for you
in front of the building
where Rimbaud stayed briefly?
You focused and shot, and later
when it was developed, the place
had no special look about it at all,
you couldn't even see the plaque.

Cocteau choking himself. Of the unexpected show that's what
you remember. Your own hand at your throat. Then yellow chairs
stacked at the back of a restaurant. That was the same day, wasn't
it? It was raining again and through rows of blue windows we
watched people rushing down the Métro steps as we sipped our
coffee.

In the mornings in rue Daguerre
you stopped in to see the hummus man.

Here we go to
the Hummus Man,
the Hummus Man,
to the Hummus Man,
so early in the morning.
Greek, he was working on his English
and doing pretty well.
Then the Asian guys at the green market.
They tolerated your bad French and spoke
English and hated France and sold you
good tomatoes and great salad greens.
One thing after another.

Midmorning and you're both in love with each other. Waiting for
your train to Carrousel du Louvre.

And every morning over by Notre-Dame there are the cartoonists
sketching tourists one at a time, one by one, one after another,
with the patience of a farm-wife, using a rolling pin against
dough, making bread before sunrise. Though you are leaving soon
as long as you are here, every day you are one and I am one and
we are, too, and two.

Every day you are one and I am one.
Continuously, we are two.

In the Yard Facing the Ocean:
A Roots Composition

Below the surface of the sea a place full of jawless and boneless creatures breathing through gills, creatures with jaws and scales and bones and flesh, creatures all deeply, deeply rooted to the sea. Here in the yard everything is equally deeply rooted – the trees, the bushes. Strawberry tree, blooming – thick with red. California condor in black tree deeply rooted to air. Acacia, two years – a girl in tears; with deep roots. In a good year its yellow blinds you. Buckeye stands by itself with roots going down and down. Two seabirds swimming on waves, both deeply rooted to water. Skyline starts turning. Everything deeply rooted except us, and we are leaving in the morning.

Weather

Church steeple through gray mist.

Stooped figures in rags
moving slowly at dusk toward light,
casting shuffling shadows.

Digging tools lie on the ground still warm
from hands that cleaned babies, boiled potatoes,
closed the gate, and fluffed straw beds.

Smell of wet, freshly turned earth.

All of humanity is a black-and-white photograph
century after century, faces looking
out of shadows at us, nameless and dateless.
They all stay enough of the same to look alike
with the light coming first from one
direction then another, day after day.

Photograph of a Gathering of People Waving

based on an old photograph bought in a
shop at Half Moon Bay, summer, 1999

No sound, the whole thing.
Unknown folk. People waving from a hillside of ripple grass
to people below in an ongoing meadow.

Side rows of trees waving in a tide of wind,
and because what is moving is not moving,
you catch a state of stasis.

Opposite of this inactivity
you imagine distant music and buzzing and crickets
and that special hot smell of summer.

To the garden past the Bay to the meadow,
cliff sheltered with low clouds, offset by nodding thistle.
Tatter-wort and Stinking Tommy along footpath
worn down by locals. But who and why?

In the photograph itself you're now looking the other way
to unknown clusters of houses.
Where forces are balanced to near perfection.

Who could live
in such a great swollen silence and solitude?

You hear church bells
from Our Lady's Tears breaking that silence nicely
but just in the right way so silence continues
as though nothing else matters day after day.

And anyway, each face seems so familiar.

What do you do when you wave back?
You wave vigorously.
You remember your own meadow,
your cliffside and town,
photographs forgotten,
the halfhearted motion of your hand,
your grandmother's church-folk
gathering on a Sunday afternoon in saintly quietness.

You name the people
whose names are not written on the back.
You forgive them for wrapping themselves in silence.

You enter house after house and open top-floor windows
and you wave down to future generations like this.

Countryside Camp

In the blue shadow of the wagon
he's carving a stick in the shape of the knife he's using.
A cross-grained sky mass turning darker with
low clouds just overhead. Bark and leaves underfoot.
Midafternoon cotton air growing heavier.
It's darker and darker.
A lamp hangs from the side.
Inhale that sweet smell
while horse grazes in shade of marigold.
Thin dog sleeps at wife's foot.
Grass gone to seed at dusk.
And horse nibbles on round marigold,
round and round the marigold.

Wanderer in a Foreign Country

At that time, after being robbed of everything, I was a wanderer in a foreign country, waiting for a check from my own. I had no job, no position, no guitar to make music, no bed or seat of my own to rest on. At first I was grateful nobody noticed me, grateful to get through the mosquitoes, grateful I hadn't fallen out of my own composition, though I'd lost the frame. Poor people down by the river lived in shacks. Theirs were fixed positions, no upward mobility. Poor people down by the river washed clothes in the river, though they had ability beyond such work. Poor people down by the river mended sacks and made baskets. Poor people down by the river ate hog liver and guts boiled. I was in a rut but not like theirs. As I passed they looked through me toward the hillside or they crossed themselves furiously. They gave me the chills with their eyes. I also walked among the well-to-do, too. As I neared they too looked through me or, to avoid me, looked up where the church bell rang whether or not it was ringing. At other times they looked directly at me and sneered, but they never crossed themselves furiously. One day I noticed a sprinkle of cottages on a ridge. Feeling invisible by now I wanted to be noticed. A woman up there on a deck waved a lace kerchief down to me. Years ago I fell in love with a woman who wore lace all the time and who had a habit of waving to heartbroken strangers. Everybody loved her as much as I did. Unfortunately, one day she fell out of her own composition, fell and landed flat on her face. She'd been suspended from a mobile axis, and when she fell she looked back at me with fear. As she plunged there was nothing I could do to save her. I gazed at the liquid spot where she vanished, gazed so long my eyes locked, and I lost my poise and my tears stopped mid-cheek. I was depressed for weeks and therefore redesigned my own frame to make sure I too wouldn't simply one day drop. I waited for her resurrection but she never resurfaced. In this foreign country often I walked under an overpass. I often passed crowds and walked around the outskirts, up and down the river-banks. I talked to no one in particular, not counting my nods and mumblings to washerwomen and waiters, clerks and clergy. I appeared poor but was unacceptable as poor, though my clothes grew dirty and I smelled. I could not imagine taking off my clothes and washing them in the river – though I should have. I couldn't go down and help the poor beat garments against the rocks. They would not have accepted me. Even the priests looked the other way. I wandered in that distant country for forty days and forty nights total. Every day I checked with the American Express office. Nothing. Nothing came. Then on the forty-first day the clerk handed me my check and said, This may or may not be for you but I have no one else to give it to. So he gave my check to me. And I cashed it, and outside to myself said: I'm sorry for the duress you've felt these forty days and forty nights, goodbye lonely stranger, we loved having you among us, go home in peace.

Part Three

In My Own Language

We can't cut this timber.
The convicts, with dreams of freedom,
gave it all they had. They
couldn't cut it. Little corrals
run all along here, no longer
used, cove converted, and also gone
the river running through here
fished by folk from Mono Lake,
and mining gone, too, but we can mine
meaning and that action stands
up pretty well, like black roots
around a tree planted incorrectly.
A posse fought hard here,
bullets flying everywhere
even knocking down an occasional orange
from a tree in that long row of orange
trees in the iron Santa Cruz sunlight.
It's a tight situation.
I move things around to make rock and tree,
water and land, connect
in their own language, but
only as I learn to speak it.

Why Wait? Do It Now

1. ON BEING LATE

I'm still in bed.
A red light glows under my bed.

2. ON BRIGHTNESS AND YOU

I come home with roses.
I leave home with roses.

The road was narrow and not much traveled.

3. AFTER ALL IS SAID

I place raw red snapper on a bright blue plate.

September and the smell of pressed grapes.

4. SOME OF THE THINGS ROSE LEFT

I wait outside my own red door, knocking,
optimistic, forever optimistic.

Do Nothing Till You Hear from Me

Motionlessly, waiting

Not that I meant to tell you

You're making your plans

More likely the actual things

In my absence. You find yourself

Facts do not solidify us

In my absence I imagine you in a stillness
not meant to be spontaneous
                                        though it is

Not that I meant for you to sit still,
motionlessly, waiting,
not that I meant to tell you anything.
Not that I meant to bring anything back
or take anything away,
certainly not you from yourself.

I hear your voice.
You're making your plans for action.

More likely the things you might have done
were the actual things you did
in my absence. You find yourself clearly.

I know you puzzle over when I will return.

I am somebody's son, somebody's husband.
You are somebody's daughter, somebody's wife.
These facts do not solidify us
as much as we might hope.

I hear you speaking even in the silence I created.
In my absence I imagine you in a stillness
hard to explain – it's like a moment acted in a play.
Acted because it's not meant to be spontaneous
though nonetheless it's sincere.

Gracelessness Recaptured as Grace

... to reduce the distinction
between what is in here and is out there...

It is as though the line
does not stop. Once drawn on the sheet
it continues beyond borders.
That is why I lease myself out loosely.
Wind blows all night.
In the morning nothing is seen moving,
         nothing not moving.

What Is a Symbol?

A bird is flying north across the white sky.
It meant to go in a different direction, possibly south.

The girl tries me on for size and sleeps on my arm,
and a halo floats over my head and I have no say.

I am the piano and the piano is playing
without me, and it's slowly Saturday. Sit down.

A monkey weeping at the screen door.
A man suspended in water and stars.

In my life important things continue to
hide themselves like ferrets.

What's beneath her fear and suspicion?
What's beneath her fear and suspicion?

Does she expect me to put her up?
Up where? In the bunk bed, in the attic, on the roof?

Once set in motion, dancing continues
without bodies, and treetops wave gently.

We'll do the museums, see movies, and walk in the park.
She hasn't touched her food.

Sit in the white chair and eat a turnip, and anyway,
what's beyond the open house and the yard?

Seeds planted back then come up now as marble.
It's all about the person behind you, not you.

I don't know why but she reminds me of confetti.
Finally her husband finds out through her mother.

The blind mule watching the pregnant woman
sipping wine regrets the dead grass.

Her bridal flowers left on the table are white chickens
with red faces, so sit down and eat a tangerine.

Sit down.

First Night of Spring

Each screaming mouth coming out toothless, bloody,
offers a black hole full of churning.

A calm center holds everything
together but the two eyes tell you nothing.

Outside at the hospital wall
something is scratching, deeply involved in a struggle.

Love Letter

I see through you. I am your wallflower.

The ground crawler finds the cracks
in the house and enters.

It comes naturally like a gathering at the river.
You give birth. It comes naturally.

We gently turn them back toward brighter light.

With my ugly white child on your black knee,
you see through me.

All eyes, for now, on us. People you invited
over, shoulder to shoulder, are zombies

under a bloody sky. I am your storm
at sea. I bleed. They do not love you.

They strip and run wild, self-obsessed. I see
through them, I see through you.

Long After You Are Ashes

In the yard the tree is changing from what it was
to what one day it will be,
changing like your insane brother
changed years ago from fun to blunt to brutal.

With good reason, I am the tree out front.
You planted me years ago by the driveway.
I am your brother with limbs and leaves.
Attended and unattended, I will grow,
in seasons with sun and rain,
and slowly change and change.

The Play of Real Life

From down here, oops, *balcon*. She walks erect,
which accents them even more.

She screams as he runs a sword through the other guy.
It's only a stage but it counts.

She gives birth, she gives her all,
yet the child in the second act looks nothing like her.

Cosmic bad casting but it's too late to start over.

On the Beach

The whole thing more likely a shuffling effect —

It may be a real horse. Very likely
two men covered, providing four legs,

clopping around, up and down the beach

as the ocean sings silver and white to blue.
Or is the music frozen waiting to restart?

to scatter earlier prints left in suspect sand.

You and Others

When they gather under trees they all sway
in the same way. Doesn't matter how
crowded. Electric lights glowing above
their heads. No match for brightness of sun.
You stand aside watching, not them
but your own sea, not trees but
your own hands on the table.
You touch the branch broken
from a tree as a spirit. In the distance
allowed by a certain calmness coming
over you, church bells ring in the Roman village
spaced so that each echo has its own say and pleasure.

Three Figures in an Interior

What's so special about shooting an animal?

You are making the motions of what passes for stillness.
Electricity gone, I light candles.
You stumble through the house,
find your shotgun and red hunting jacket.
As usual, I will not go with you.
I cover daughter sleeping with legs apart.
You get a head start. Drive safely.
You will return with blood dripping all the way.
My plan is to pass my time on
to anyone interested in taking it.

The Art of Sitting in a Chair

She is at half rest in the practice of a simple art.
She is by the window washed in brown shade.

Long skirt down to her ankles,
she is sitting with legs crossed, arms folded, head tilted
to the right — her right, my left.

Can she hear the boy plucking the strings of the banjo?
How tender of the old man to teach the kid.

But knowing the rest is not resting.

Birds humming go their iridescent way.

The People Next Door

The phone ringing in a sandstorm.
That's what it's like.
Things brought down on the wind.
The best I can tell you is go through the alphabet.
Somebody screaming.
Pots and pans rattling over there,
cooker and coffeepot, kettle and skillet
banging together. Or is that singing?

The Hat Lady in the Parlor Window

Upper-left corner of the parlor window broken.
For three days her beloved gone.
A thick grayness passing in the sky...
something rotten, sailing in the air...
  There goes Mrs. Y stepping along.
Tapping three times with her wedding ring.
  Careful, the whole thing might fall.
Down on her knees, feeling the sharp –
"Crawl under, Luke. Maybe she's stuck."
In that dream last night the dog without a head.
Three vacant rooms left in the basement and a sign.
East or west the view you nearly remembered.
Baby on the front porch gnawing her own hip.
And that time she was going down the front steps
one at a time, in manner of an old dog.
  Unlike the dog to wander off...
"Miss V! Better come quick!"
Mrs. Y looking critically in the mirror at herself.
"I don't think it's *me*, Victoria."
  Joe and his wife Agnes, kids grown and gone...
"Let me think about it, Victoria."
The boy on his knees: "She ain't moving, Miss V."
Holding tightly to the railing, looking at Luke –
  Almost to capacity – three left.
But hard to keep anybody down there, the dampness.

Nothing wrong with sharing a bathroom.
I just wouldn't want to do it myself.
Quiet today – not even the Fletchers' radio.
Clock in the foyer chimes hard and harder.
Damp, yes, but Charlie put in toilets and sinks
and didn't charge an arm.
Even his hired winos breaking nothing.
"What do you see under there – ?"
And Luke dragging it out by a stiff front leg.

Inside Outside

Late afternoon, who can tell?

Inside, steam from the pot of butter beans drifts outside.
From outside comes the smell of winterberries and pine.

This evening, the moon and spoon tapping,
singing and dancing.

By midnight, laughter like screams.

The Memory and the Place

Well, he says, I no longer need your slide-door
and your stairway to that room of no light.
She says, Absence is loud in my life but I live well with noise.
It's a natural element and more than I ever meant.
Remember we talked quietly inside by the fire, waiting
for summer, and remember the darkness we walked in
and the snow freezing on purpose to what purpose?

Process and Space

You never have to know the whole story.
Binary opposites dance together.

To suggest space fully
you need to place objects in it.
Certain types of contradictions are useful.

They relocated positions of whole buildings
in order to build better compositions.

A whole coastal area emerged,
stormy muddy sky behind it.

Each eye saw something different in the tracing.

A naked child running
down the middle of a road screaming.
Everyone else fully dressed and walking.

An ancient road over the mountains
going nowhere though land lies
endlessly ahead.

Certain types of contradictions are useful.
A strange transparent figure on a white horse
galloping across sand

wearing a peasant crucifixion.
It's riding into a sunrise
of hazy light along the horizon,
shore trimmed with a thin line of green.

It all whips back and forth
like broken jalousies
in a halfhearted storm.

Unknown Presence

How to name what is unnameable.
The long road of history right up till now.
Think about Robert Johnson's deal with the Devil.
Unnameable, I think of you.
I know my demise is coded in your name.

But what does Unnameable know that I don't know?
In retrospect, oh, so that's how it all adds up.
We're in a new car driving along but
if something goes wrong
out here in the middle of nowhere,
no mechanic to deal with the problem.

The deal is that moment when no one knows
who has the ball, not even he, scratched and bruised, carrying it.

So, we keep bumping into one another,
used, our keys rattling.

You leave stage and come back dancing.
And I have no choice.
Watching your high kicks with a longing
that matches your tease.

And Lil at the piano at Bob's.
A big deal for me.
We stayed up all night
listening to her play and
doing so made all mystery leave
at least for those few hours.

But the reality is, I bear the weight.
I listen to your screams coming up.
I no longer deny that
your voice and heartbeat are my own.

People are happiest when they forget.
Everyone forgot you that time in Kansas City
when Half Pint pitched high
and sang way up in a voice not his own.

Not unhappy, now I am inside *you*
crossing an imaginary stretch
as if you were an unending coastline,
too lovely to look at with the naked eye.
I couldn't have been dealt a better hand.

Reading about Rocks

This book, solid and heavy as rock,
a cousin of the earth.

Loose rock tumbling down.
At the bottom, debris, dust rising.
And constant wind sweeping the earth.
You are a cousin of earth,
the stuff of glaciers; and your brain
is made of leaves and straw and fish bones.

Say you and this kettle lake.
Say fragments, clusters, a monolith.
Rocks touching back with sediments and shale
matching your mentality to lake sludge.

Unaltered granite? Watch it alter.
Footprints in the sediments become markers.
Watch them deepen.
Watch the lifting light sift
surfaces of both solids — your hand and the rock.

The Document

I wait in the house for the arrival of an important person. I pace the floor. I think of calling to see if something has gone wrong. The person has promised to come and sign a document lying on the coffee table. I open the door and check the street. The signature will give me a greater sense of security. No fee. That's my understanding. I pick up the phone but can't remember the number. Has he misunderstood, gotten the date wrong? I pace the floor and think perhaps his signature isn't necessary, after all. Perhaps security will come without a signature. Perhaps I myself can sign and feel what I need. I know the document must be delivered to a certain office by opening time tomorrow. I pick up the document. I was wrong. The due date is today. I take out my fountain pen and sign the silly paper. There! It's done! Slowly, I put on my coat and gloves. K comes into the room and says it's too late, the office closed ten minutes ago. *You must move faster.* But, she adds, there is no great loss. The document, she says, is of no importance. Not now, never was. I say, How can that be? I signed it, it's ready to go. It will make my life safer. But K says, No, you misunderstand. The document, she says, is only a pretext to get a signature, yours or anybody's, it's an invitation to activity, part of the shudder and roar, not a secure text, only a pretend-insurance against everything you fear. K says, You may as well burn the document, it's worthless. *You're on your own. You always were.*

One Thing for Sure

One thing for sure, you are in motion.
Catalytic.
Fleet-footed, you spring forth.
Fluid, you fly.
Your motion is snappy, crisp, nimble, and kinetic.
You defy your apathetic body.
Jaunty, you tease your way all the way,
under rainbow, across rim.

And the other thing for sure, this:
you are slowing, slowing down.
Slowing to that dreamy pace,
down to a hypnotic saunter,
to a complacent crawl, to a prone groan.

But motion is what defines you.
Even after you are dead
it is the agile streak you leave in the sky,
the acrobatic stuff people remember.
How you smiled with a breezy expression
that won or lost everybody.

You always believed in one body at a time.
Your body is moving in a certain way,
rotating forward into darkness,
rotating back out of darkness.

Salt? Bodies of salt.
Salt is not the opposite of fresh,
although with water it's a different story.
I am not the opposite of you.

Pursuit.
In suit or jeans, you are in pursuit.
The habit of pursuing – as if from treetop to treetop,
as though you were crow and hawk.
You go about like map lines
joining one point to another.
Even while moving in circles
or zigzagging, you follow
your worn-out, earthbound, isometric lines.
Through flash floods and frost,
through drizzle and earthquake,
through hailstorms and pollution,
and through erosion and eruption,
you follow those lines, connecting the dots.

A two-stroke engine starts.
You are its motor.
Smell of petrol spreads across your lawn.
Crankshaft rattles, then an explosion.
Whatever is going on out there,

efficiency is not part of it.
Whatever is going on with us,
the best intelligence is not part of it.

Thorny shrubs.
Deep in the thorny shrubs sweet cherries.
How to get in and out without blood.
That is the vexing unknown.

This is how: merciless, peevish, lovely.
Black wingspread showing
the underside of white patches.
The eye moves inside the socket,
the tail flickers.

Laughing and singing.
Salty and self-serving.
Your properties.
Snappish and snippety. Your properties.
Laughing in the middle,
causing unrest.

Spring nights and shrills from the lake.
On spring nights you take these truths
because the season is easier.

In the dark yard, trills.
Which is not to say that you no longer
believe winter will come gliding back
with its hoarse croak and new plumage.

Rumors: A Family Matter

Dates escape me. At any rate Aunt Thelma lived on in grief. When Uncle Wilbur lived he cut and hacked, cut and hacked sugarcane rain or ruin. Sometimes he tracked mud in the house and Aunt Thelma gave him a piece of her mind. You can see her with fists on hips and that look. Those were just rumors you heard about the marriage. Rumor of what they did and did not do together. Not a day in life did my uncle tolerate lawyers or funerals or fakers, crude women or insurance. A tumor in his throat, he laid his life out in layers so he could see it, hear it clearly even as he coughed the thief. He lived out on a limb till he died, not a tear, not a complaint. They said he never lied to anybody. Plain as porch planks, they never accepted Relief. I mean he saw himself. It was hard to see himself but nothing else counted more. Aunt Thelma, slim as a butcher knife, and though made of firmness itself, made sure he made out a Will to relieve her of fear. The Will was dated and not much but this is many years later and dates escape me. And although Aunt Thelma lived on in grief, it's not too late to remember with kindness.

The Painting after Lunch

It wasn't working. Didn't look back. Needed something else. So I went out. After lunch I saw it in a different light, like a thing emerging from behind a fever bush, something reaching the senses with the smell of seaweed boiling, and as visible as yellow snowdrops on black earth. Tasted it too, on the tongue Jamaica pepper. To the touch, a velvet flower. Dragging and scumming, I gave myself to it stroke after stroke. It kept coming in bits and fits, fragments and snags. I even heard it singing but in the wrong key like a deranged bird in wild cherries, having the time of its life.

Film and Flesh

I was watching a movie
about myself
when I suddenly saw
someone else,
something else — a nightmare figure,
maybe human, maybe not,
maybe the star of a dark carnival —
on the set, entirely realistic,

assume my identity, walking away
with me, explaining nothing
even as he spoke over his shoulder,
saying it's okay; I also play nurses,
matrons, schoolmistresses, doctors.

It's okay? Is it Saturday night and Sunday morning
all the time? Was it okay
with Ava Gardner, in Singapore?

I can sing. I have a brain, muscle and hair,
gastric glands and two eyes. I work
the garden, I am liquid and membrane.
I am not film. I am living, I say.

Waiting for Sweet Betty

The sweetest waiting is waiting for Sweet Betty.
Pretty but messy, they say. Bird's-eye view
sees a blanket of shimmering pink and white
with green pods in sharp brightness.

Down beneath in the flower's cool shade,
in scattered shadows so dark, I wait
in uneasy restfulness,
waiting through sun and snow.
There's much to wait for.
I wait for plum rock to turn a darker purple.
I wait for the unmistakable black in white people to show.
I wait for black people to catch windflowers.
The sweetest waiting, though, is waiting for Sweet Betty.

Waiting is what I do.
I waited nine months to be born.
I meant to say something else.
In sleep I wait to wake.
I wait for the right moment.
I wait for the birds to finish with their nest and fussing.
I wait for the right book with the right cover.
I wait for the grass to take deep root.
I wait to see the bushes reach their fullness.
I wait for the grocer to fill my sack.

I wait in the hallway against the wall.
I wait for my students to finish the exam.
I wait for my students to start talking.
I wait for payday and I wait for the lottery.
I wait at the lake for the boat.
I wait offstage to have my say.
I wait at the zoo for the ram to stand up.

I wait in waiting rooms, rest homes, recovery rooms.
I wait patiently as a patient in ward after ward.
I wait for the witch doctor to tell me something – anything.
I wait like a mechanic watching oil drain into a pan.

I wait for the axis to shift and the system to set.
I wait for the matrix to absorb the math of itself.
I wait for the big crunch to meet the big bang.
I wait like an astronaut strapped in a plastic seat.
I wait a light-year for light to travel through chaos.

I wait in Georgia sad on a base and in Illinois with a dime.
I wait in New York with a subway token and a briefcase.
Now we're recounting personal history.
I wait in fatigues in line in Texas, waiting and waiting.
I wait in the airport in Ghana and Liberia.
I wait in France for my identity papers.

I wait in the train station in Germany and in Holland.
I wait in Italy hoping time will stop for a rest.
I wait in Colorado and California without skis.
I await a Nebraska driving test and I fail.
I wait in the air and on the high seas, waiting calmly.
Who can tell how long I wait?

I wait for Skunk Bush to stop smelling.
I wait for Wandering Jenny to stop climbing the house,
to stop flying around and around the clouds
trying to kiss the upside-down boy. I wait for her
to move in another direction, to rest on a rock.

I wait the sweetest waiting of all —
I wait for Sweet Betty and she won't bloom till next year,
but she *will* bloom next year.

Thomas Eakins's Delaware River Paintings

Land and water make love all night all day.

The moment of silence before the explosion.
Then the explosion, then the silence again.
The men know not to talk but the guns can't help it.

The objective: the elusive bird.

In the Neck swamp-cabbage stink,
pigs and muddy dogs watching the sky.
The polemen push and the shooters shoot.

This one poleman, a black man — lean and strong —
stands barefoot on the back end pushing,
and suddenly distracted by a noise in the underbrush,
he looks this way,
motionlessly,
as if shot dead by a camera.

They say he's from farther south.

Dogs and men show sharp interest
as the elusive marsh bird falls
gracelessly along the sky.

Shooters, white men all,
standing in their boats quietly.

Polemen, black men all,
all pushing them quietly along the river.

Will Schuster and the nameless black man come here often.
Will Schuster shoots and the black man rows.

Tom, too, goes for the kill, the fix dead-on.

Land and water make love all day all night.

Thomas Eakins and the Photograph of a Man in Motion

Something in us spins out of control, colliding with frame-by-frame flickering of our exhausted histories, yet remains motionless. Our best hopes look sweet like progression, like forward motion, and maybe they are. He gives us hope as he progresses as calmly and forcefully as a ship reaching port but he has no docking permit. He may also be in the wrong city, in the wrong season, yet the implication of the sequence is undeniable.

About the Author

Clarence Major is a prizewinning poet whose first collection, *Swallow the Lake,* won the National Council on the Arts Award in 1970. He is also the author of nine novels, including *Dirty Bird Blues; My Amputations* (Western States Book Award, 1986); *Such Was the Season* (Literary Guild Selection, 1987); and *Painted Turtle: Woman with Guitar* (*New York Times* "Notable Book of the Year" citation, 1988). Author of ten books of poetry, Major was a 1999 finalist for the National Book Award for *Configurations: New and Selected Poems, 1958-1998.* Major's poetry also earned him a 1971 New York Cultural Foundation prize. He is a contributor to more than a hundred periodicals and anthologies. He has served as literary judge for the National Endowment for the Arts, National Book Awards, and many state and cultural arts agencies. He has read his poetry at the Guggenheim Museum, the Folger Theatre, and in hundreds of universities, theaters, and cultural centers in the United States and Europe. In Yugoslavia he represented the United States in 1975 at the International Poetry Festival. He is also the editor of several anthologies widely used in university classes. Clarence Major teaches American literature at the University of California, Davis.

The Chinese character for poetry is made up of two parts: "word" and "temple." It also serves as pressmark for Copper Canyon Press.

Founded in 1972, Copper Canyon Press remains dedicated to publishing poetry exclusively, from Nobel laureates to new and emerging authors. The Press thrives with the generous patronage of readers, writers, booksellers, librarians, teachers, students, and funders – everyone who shares the conviction that poetry invigorates the language and sharpens our appreciation of the world.

PUBLISHERS' CIRCLE

The Allen Foundation for the Arts

Lannan Foundation

National Endowment for the Arts

EDITORS' CIRCLE

Thatcher Bailey

The Breneman Jaech Foundation

Cynthia Hartwig and Tom Booster

Port Townsend Paper Company

Target Stores

Emily Warn and Daj Oberg

Washington State Arts Commission

For information and catalogs:

COPPER CANYON PRESS
Post Office Box 271
Port Townsend, Washington 98368
360/385-4925
www.coppercanyonpress.org

Set in Mendoza, a typeface designed by
José Mendoza y Almeida. Book design
and composition by Valerie Brewster,
Scribe Typography. Printed on archival-
quality Glatfelter Author's Text at
McNaughton & Gunn, Inc.